The BIG BOOK of Belly Laugh Jokes, Riddles, and Puns for Kids

The BIG BOOK of Belly Laugh Jokes, Riddles, and Puns for Kids

Illustrated by Bethany Straker

Sky Pony Press
New York, New York

Special thanks to:
Bethany Straker for her fabulous illustrations
and Kylie Brien for her silly, funny jokes

Sky Pony Press books may be purchased in bulk at special discounts for sales promotion,
corporate gifts, fund-raising, or educational purposes. Special editions can also be created
to specifications. For details, contact the Special Sales Department, Sky Pony Press,
307 West 36th Street, 11th Floor, New York, NY 10018 or info@skyhorsepublishing.com.

Sky Pony® is a registered trademark of Skyhorse Publishing, Inc.®,
a Delaware corporation.

Visit our website at www.skyponypress.com.

10 9 8 7 6 5 4 3 2 1

This product conforms to CPSIA 2008

Library of Congress Cataloging-in-Publication Data

Cover design by Kai Texel

Print ISBN: 978-1-5107-7284-7
E-Book ISBN: 978-1-5107-7357-8

Printed in the United States of America

Portions of the this book were previously published as
Belly Laugh Jokes for Kids (ISBN: 978-1-63450-156-9) and
Belly Laugh Riddles and Puns for Kids (ISBN: 978-1-5107-1198-3)

**Q: What's the difference between
a piano and a fish?**
A: You can tune a piano but
you can't tuna fish.

Q: How do you get spoiled milk?
A: From a pampered cow.

Q: Why was the painting sent to prison?
A: Because it was framed.

**Q: Why did the chicken
cross the playground?**
A: To get to the other slide.

Q: Why do bees have sticky hair?
A: Because they use honeycombs.

**Q: What do you call cheese that
doesn't belong to you?**
A: Nacho cheese!

Q: Where do cows go on Friday night?
A: To the *MOOO*vie theater.

Q: Why can't the bicycle stand up by itself?
A: Because it's two-tired!

Q: What did one toilet say to the other?
A: You look a tad flushed.

Q: What did Cinderella say when her photos did not show up?
A: Someday my prints will come!

Q: Why couldn't the pirate play cards?
A: Because he was sitting
on the deck!

Q: What did one ocean say to the other ocean?
A: Nothing, it just waved.

**Q: What did the janitor say when
he jumped out of the closet?**
A: Supplies!

**Q: What is an astronaut's
favorite place on a computer?**
A: The Space bar!

Q: What did one eye say to the other eye?
A: Don't look now, but something
in between us smells.

Q: Why did the dinosaur cross the road?
A: Because the chicken joke wasn't invented yet.

Q: What is a tree's favorite kind of soda?
A: Root Beer.

Q: What do you get when you cross a thief with an alligator?
A: A crook-odile.

Q: What do you call a snail on a ship?
A: A snailor.

Q: What kind of pet makes the loudest noise?
A: A trumpet.

Q: What's a toad's favorite kind of drink?
A: Croak-a-cola.

Q: What is a sheep's favorite kind of dance?
A: The baaaaaah-let.

**Q: What is a ghost's favorite
position to play in soccer?**
A: Ghoulie.

**Q: Why did Cinderella get kicked off the
soccer team?**
A: She was always running away from the ball.

**Q: Why did the golfer have on
two pairs of pants?**
A: In case he got a hole-in-one.

Q: What do baseball teams and pancakes have in common?

A: They both need a good batter.

Q: What do you call a guy who never farts in public?

A: A private tutor.

Q: Why did the ballerina quit?

A: It was tutu hard.

**Q: Why was the policeman
at the baseball game?**

A: He heard someone stole a base.

Q: Why can't your nose be 12 inches long?

A: Because then it would be a foot!

**Q: Why did the farmer ride
his horse into town?**

A: The horse was too heavy to carry.

Q: What type of haircuts do bees get?
A: Buzz cuts!

Q: What animal does a dentist like best?
A: Molar bears.

Q: Why was the doctor angry?
A: He ran out of patients.

Q: Did you hear the one about the germ?
A: Never mind then. I don't want
to spread it around.

Q: What's the best thing to put in a pie?
A: Your teeth.

**Q: Why can't you tell a joke when you're
standing on ice?**
A: Because it might crack-up!

Q: Where do snowmen keep their money?
A: In a snow bank.

**Q: What did the baby corn say
to the mom corn?**
A: Where's pop corn?

Q: What did the stamp say to the envelope?
A: Stick with me and we'll go places!

**Q: What kind of keys do kids like
to carry around?**
A: Cookies.

Q: What is a sleeping bull called?
A: A bull-dozer.

Q: Why are teddy bears never hungry?
A: They're always stuffed.

Q: Why are fish so smart?
A: Because they live in schools.

**Q: What happened to the lion after
he ate the comedian?**
A: He felt funny.

**Q: What do you get when you mix
a snake and a pie?**
A: A pie-thon.

Q: Why didn't the monkey believe the tiger?
A: She thought he was lion.

Q: What animal has more lives than a cat?
A: Frogs—they croak every night!

Q: What dog keeps the best time?
A: A watch dog!

**Q: What did the buffalo say to his son
when he left for work?**
A: Bison!

Q: What is a cat's favorite color?
A: Purrrr-ple.

**Q: What could be worse than raining
cats and dogs?**
A: Hailing taxi cabs.

**Q: Why are cats good at
video games?**

A: Because they have nine lives.

Q: What did the detective duck do?

A: He quacked the case.

**Q: What time is it when a rhino
sits on the fence?**

A: Time to get a new fence.

**Q: How do you stop an elephant
from charging?**
A: You take away all his
credit cards.

**Q: What kind of dog loves to take
bubble baths?**
A: A shampoodle.

Q: What kind of markets should dogs avoid?
A: Flea markets.

Q: Why do birds fly south for the winter?
A: It's too far to walk.

Q: What is a funny chicken called?
A: A comedi-hen.

Q: Why are graveyards so noisy?
A: Because of all the coffin.

Q: When is it bad luck to meet a black cat?
A: When you're a mouse.

Q: What is a scarecrow's favorite food?
A: Straw-berries.

Q: How do you make a witch itch?
A: Take away the *W*.

Knock, knock.
Who's there?
Leaf.
Leaf who?
Leaf me alone!

Knock, knock
Who's there?
Woo.
Woo who?
Calm down, it's just a joke.

Q: Why are pirates named pirates?
A: Because they arrrrg!

Knock, knock.

Who's there?

Theodore.

Theodore who?

Theodore won't open. Let me in!

Knock, knock.

Who's there.

Police.

Police who?

Police let me in. It's cold out here.

Q: What type of music do balloons hate?
A: Pop music, of course.

Q: What has forty feet and sings?
A: The school choir!

Q: What is the most musical part of a fish?
A: Its scales.

Q: What kind of plates do they use on Mars?
A: Flying saucers.

Q: How do you get straight As?
A: Use a ruler.

Q: What do librarians take with them when they go fishing?
A: Bookworms.

Q: Why does the clock in the cafeteria run slow?
A: It went back for seconds.

Q: Why didn't the sun go to college?
A: Because it already had a million degrees.

Q: What is the capital of Washington?
A: *W.*

Q: What did they do at the Boston Tea Party?
A: I don't know. I wasn't invited.

Q: What do Alexander the Great and Kermit the Frog have in common?
A: The same middle name.

Q: Why was the math book sad?
A: Because it had too many problems.

Q: Why do seagulls fly over the sea?
A: Because if they flew over the bay they would
be called bagels.

Q: What color socks do bears usually wear?
A: None! They usually have bear feet.

Q: What does a cloud wear under its raincoat?
A: Thunderwear!

Q: What do you call a grizzly bear out in the rain?

A: A drizzly bear.

Q: What steps do you take if a tiger is running toward you?

A: Big ones.

Q: What did the girl pig say to the boy pig?

A: You are so *hamsome*!

Q: What is better than a talking dinosaur?
A: A spelling bee.

Q: What did Santa say when Mrs. Claus
asked about the weather?
A: It looks like reindeer.

Q: What kind of tree can you fit in your hand?
A: A palm tree.

Q: Why didn't the skeleton play golf?
A: His heart wasn't in it.

Q: How much did the pirate pay
for his earrings?
A: A buccaneer.

Q: Why are there fences around graveyards?
A: Because people are just dying to get in.

Q: Why are pianos hard to open?

A: Because the keys are inside.

Q: What did the duck say when he finished shopping?

A: Put it on my bill.

Q: What do you call a gorilla wearing earmuffs?

A: Anything you want. He can't hear you.

Q: Where do you send a frog to get glasses?
A: The hoptometrist.

Q: What do you get when you cross a snowman and a vampire?
A: Frostbite.

Q: How do prisoners call each other?
A: On their cell phones.

Q: Where does a polar bear go to vote?
A: The North Poll.

Q: Why don't skeletons get into fights?
A: They don't have the guts.

Q: What did the judge say when a skunk wandered into the courtroom?
A: Odor in the court.

Knock, knock
Who's there?
Arthur.
Arthur who?
Arthur any more cookies left?

Q: Why was the computer so chilly?
A: It left its windows open.

Q: What kind of apple has a short temper?
A: A crab apple.

Knock, knock

Who's there?

Nobel.

Nobel who?

I had to knock because there was nobel!

Q: What do you get when you cross a cow with a trampoline.

A: A milk shake.

Q: What's the king of the pencil box?

A: The ruler.

Q: What's at the end of everything?

A: A *G*.

Q: What do you call a famous fish?

A: A starfish.

Q: What do you get if you cross a parrot with a shark?

A: A bird that will talk your ear off.

Q: How do trains hear?

A: Through their engineers.

Q: What do you call a ghost's true love?

A: His ghoul-friend.

Q: Why didn't the girl take the bus home?

A: Because her mom would make
her take it back.

Q: How do you talk to a giant?

A: Use big words!

Q: What does a nosy pepper do?

A: Gets jalapeño business!

Q: What dog can jump higher than a building?

A: Any dog. Buildings can't jump.

**Q: What lies at the bottom of the
sea and shakes.**

A: A nervous shipwreck.

Q: Why can't fishermen be generous?

A: Because their business makes them shellfish.

Q: Why do cats make terrible storytellers?

A: Because they only have one tail.

Q: How do you fix a cracked pumpkin?
A: With a pumpkin patch.

Q: Why do dogs run in circles?
A: Because it's hard to run in squares.

Q: What is big and gray and has sixteen wheels?
A: An elephant on roller skates.

Q: What do you get if you cross a math teacher and a clock?
A: Arithma-ticks.

Q: What did one volcano say to the other?
A: I lava you!

Q: Why do bears have hairy coats?
A: Fur protection.

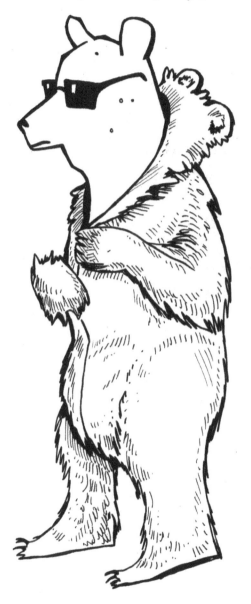

Q: Why are skeletons so calm?

A: Because nothing gets under their skin.

Q: What did the beaver say to the tree?

A: It's been nice gnawing you.

Q: What do you call a bee who's having a bad hair day?

A: A Frisbee.

Q: Why wouldn't the shrimp share the treasure he found?
A: He was a little shellfish.

Q: How does a lion like his meat?
A: Medium roar.

Q: What kind of horse goes out after dark?
A: Nightmares!

Q: How does an octopus go to war?
A: Well-armed.

Q: What side of the cheetah has the most spots?
A: The outside.

Q: What did the painter say to the wall?
A: I've got you covered!

Q: What do you do with a sick boat?
A: You take it to the doc.

Q: What's the best way to carve wood?
A: Whittle by whittle.

Q: What's a bunny's favorite kind of dance?
A: Hip-hop!

Q: Why didn't the watermelons get married?
A: Because they cantaloupe.

Q: What does a panda ghost eat?
A: Bam-boo.

Q: Where did George Washington keep his armies?
A: In his sleevies.

Q: Did you guys hear about the circus fire?

A: It was in-tents.

Q: What did one hat say to the other?

A: You stay here—I'll go on ahead.

Q: What did the worker at the rubber band factory say when he lost his job?

A: Oh snap.

Q: What washes up on tiny beaches?
A: Microwaves.

Q: Why did the skeleton go to the party alone?
A: He had no body to go with him.

Q: What's a butterfly's favorite subject in school?
A: Mothematics.

Q: Why didn't the two 4s eat lunch?
A: Because they already 8.

Q: What is the difference between a teacher and a steam engine?
A: One says, "Spit out that gum immediately!" and the other says, "Chew! Chew! Chew!"

Q: What makes more noise than a dinosaur?
A: Two dinosaurs.

Q: How does a mouse feel after a shower?
A: Squeaky clean!

**Q: What's the difference between
a dog and a flea?**
A: A dog can have fleas but a flea can't have
dogs.

Q: What is a cat's favorite button on the remote?
A: Paws.

Q: How do rabbits travel?
A: By hare-plane.

Q: What do you get when you cross a kangaroo and an elephant?
A: Great big holes all over Australia.

Q: What is a vampire's favorite part of a guitar?
A: The neck.

Q: What do you get if you throw butter?
A: A butterfly.

Q: What do you call a fly with no wings?
A: A walk.

Q: What do you give an alien?
A: Some space.

**Q: What's the difference between
a car and a bull?**

A: A car only has one horn.

Q: Why were the apple and orange alone?
A: Because the banana split.

Q: How do you keep a chicken in suspense?
A: I'll tell you later.

Q: What do you call an elephant in a phone booth?

A: Stuck.

Q: What goes down but never goes up?

A: A rhino in an elevator.

Q: Why do elephants have trunks?

A: Because they'd look pretty silly with glove compartments.

Q: What do cats have that other animals don't?
A: Kittens.

Q: Why do skunks celebrate Valentine's Day?
A: They're scent-imental.

Q: What's the best place to grow flowers in school?
A: In kindergarten.

Q: How do you get a squirrel to like you?
A: Act like a nut!

**Q: What do you get when you cross
a teacher and a vampire?**
A: Lots of blood tests.

Q: Why did the dalmatian go to the eye doctor?
A: Because he kept seeing spots.

Q: What has the fur of a dog, the whiskers of a dog, and the tail of a dog but is not a dog?

A: A puppy.

Q: Why is the ocean always grumpy?

A: You would be grumpy too if you had crabs on your bottom.

Q: What happened to the hamburger who missed a lot of school?

A: He had a lot of ketchup time.

Q: How does a scientist freshen her breath?
A: With experi-mints!

Q: What kind of shoes do spies wear?
A: Sneakers.

Q: What do you call an elephant at the North Pole?
A: Lost.

Q: How do beavers get online?

A: They log on.

Q: Where do you find giant snails?

A: On the end of giants' fingers.

**Q: What do you get when you cross
a stream and a brook?**

A: Wet feet.

Q: What kind of stories do the ship captain's children like to hear?
A: Ferry tales.

Q: What do you give a sick frog?
A: A hoperation.

Q: How do penguins get to school?
A: On their ice-cycles.

Q: What does a brain do when it sees a friend across the street?

A: Gives it a brain wave.

Q: What did the lettuce say to the celery?

A: Quit stalking me!

Q: Which weighs more: a ton of feathers or a ton of bricks?

A: Neither. They both weigh a ton.

Q: What do you call an angry pea?
A: Grum-pea.

Q: What sport do elephants like to play?
A: Squash.

Q: Why do toadstools grow so close together?
A: Because they don't need mushroom.

Q: When is a car not a car?

A: When it turns into a garage.

Q: What do you get when you put a fish and an elephant together?

A: Swimming trunks.

Q: What do you call a surgeon with eight arms?

A: A doctopus.

Q: Why did the belt go to jail?
A: Because it held up a pair of pants.

Q: What is the center of gravity?
A: *V*.

Q: What sort of star is dangerous?
A: A shooting star.

Q: When does a cart come before the horse?
A: In the dictionary.

Q: What do you do with a blue whale?
A: Try to cheer him up.

Q: What kind of key opens a banana?
A: A monkey.

Q: How are false teeth like stars?

A: They come out at night!

Q: How many books can you fit in an empty backpack?

A: One. After that it's not empty anymore.

Q: Why is the letter G scary?

A: It turns a host into a ghost.

Q: Which letters are not in the alphabet?

A: The ones in the mail, of course.

**Q: Which are the strongest creatures
in the ocean?**

A: Muscles.

Q: Which bean is the most intelligent?

A: The human bean.

Knock, knock
Who's there?
Wooden shoe.
Wooden shoe who?
**Wooden shoe like to hear
another joke?**

Q: Did you hear the joke about oatmeal?
A: It's a lot of mush.

Q: When do astronauts have lunch?
A: At launch time.

Q: If a meteorite hits a planet, what do we call the ones that miss?

A: Meteowrongs.

Q: What is the difference between weather and climate?

A: You can't weather a tree but you can climate.

Q: What happens when it rains cats and dogs?

A: You have to be careful not to step in a poodle.

Q: How can you tell a vampire has a cold?
A: He starts coffin.

Q: What did one elevator say to another?
A: I think I'm coming down with something.

Q: Why do witches wear name tags?
A: So they know which one is witch.

Q: What do you call a camel with no humps?
A: Humphrey.

Q: Why are frogs so happy?
A: They eat whatever bugs them.

Q: What do you call a lazy baby kangaroo?
A: A pouch potato.

Q: What do you call a really old ant?
A: An antique.

Q: What do you call it when it rains chickens and ducks?
A: Fowl weather.

Q: What do you call it when you put three ducks in a box?
A: A box of quackers.

**Q: What do you think of that
new diner on the moon?**
A: Food was good, but there really
wasn't much atmosphere.

Q: What did the pony say when he fell over?
A: I've fallen and I can't giddy up!

Q: Do zombies eat donuts with their fingers?
A: No—they eat their fingers afterward!

Q: What do stylish frogs wear?
A: Jumpsuits.

Q: What do you call a bear with no teeth?
A: A gummy bear.

Q: Why couldn't the mouse find a roommate?
A: Because his house was such a hole in the wall.

Q: Why did the ape sell his banana shop?
A: Because he was tired of all the
monkey business.

Q: How does a farmer count his cows?
A: With a cow-culator.

Q: How do you make an octopus laugh?
A: With ten-tickles!

Q: What did the caterpillar do when he lost his wallet?

A: He totally bugged out!

Q: Why do ducks make the best spies?

A: They're great at quacking codes.

Q: What do you say when someone throws a duck at a duck?

A: Duck!

Q: Why did the kid bring a ladder to school?
A: Because he wanted to go to high school.

Q: How do you fire a math teacher?
A: Tell her she's history.

Q: What do you call a student who is great at subtracting, multiplication, and division but can't add?
A: A total failure!

Q: Where does one find Canada?

A: On a map.

Q: What do you call a blind dinosaur?

A: Doyouthinkhesawus.

Q: What did the alien say to the cat?

A: Take me to your litter.

Q: How do you turn a normal scientist into a mad scientist?

A: Step on her toes.

Q: What did the robot's family put on his tombstone?

A: Rust in peace.

Q: How did the giant know Jack was coming?

A: He could hear Jack and the beans talk.

Q: What did one plate say to the other plate?
A: Dinner's on me.

Q: What's the difference between a red light and a green light?
A: The color, obviously!

Q: What kind of flower grows on your face?
A: Tulips!

**Q: What is the most musical part
of a chicken?**
A: The drumstick.

Q: What kind of driver doesn't need a license?
A: A screwdriver.

Q: Why was the donut at the dentist?
A: It needed filling!

Q: How did the captain of the Titanic know his ship was going down?
A: He had a sinking feeling.

Q: Why couldn't the Tin Man play cards with Dorothy and the Scarecrow?
A: They were playing Hearts.

Q: Why can't matches play baseball?
A: One strike and they're out!

Q: How do you make a bandstand?
A: Take away their chairs.

**Q: What do you get when you cross
a library and a golfer?**
A: Book clubs.

Q: What kind of herb is green and sings?
A: Elvis Parsley.

Q: Why did the tiger eat the tightrope walker?
A: He wanted a well-balanced meal.

Q: When should you buy a pet bird?
A: When it's going cheep!

Q: Why was the baker so rich?
A: He made a lot of dough.

Q: How do angels answer their telephones?
A: "Halo!"

Q: How do you learn to be a judge?
A: Through trial and error.

Q: What is a doc-doc joke?
A: A knock-knock joke with a cold.

Q: Why do mimes make bad witnesses?
A: They can never really say what happened.

Q: What do farmers plant in their sofas?
A: Couch potatoes.

Q: What's gray, has wings, and gives money to baby elephants?
A: The tusk fairy.

Q: Why do dragons sleep all day?
A: So they can fly knights.

Q: Where do baby ghosts go during the day?
A: The dayscare center.

Q: When do ghosts usually appear?
A: Before someone screams.

Q: Which is faster, hot or cold?
A: Hot. You can always catch cold.

Knock, knock
Who's there?
Wire.
Wire who?
Wire you asking me that again?
I just told you.

Q: Why did the banana go to the doctor?
A: Because he wasn't peeling well.

Q: What do you call an illegally parked frog?
A: Toad.

Q: What does an evil hen lay?
A: Deviled eggs.

Q: What do you do when a sink knocks at your door?

A: You let that sink in.

Q: What is a can opener that doesn't work called?

A: A can't opener.

Q: What do you call someone who points out the obvious?

A: Someone who points out the obvious.

Q: Who is a penguin's favorite aunt?

A: Aunt Arctica!

Knock, knock

Who's there?

Wanda.

Wanda who?

Wanda hang out with me right now?

Q: What kind of books do bunnies read?

A: Ones with hoppy endings.

Knock, knock
Who's there?
Howl.
Howl who?
**Howl you know it's really me
unless you let me in?**

Q: What does bread do on vacation?
A: Loaf around.

Q: What do you call a ghost's parents?
A: Transparents.

Q: What streets do ghosts usually haunt?
A: Dead ends.

Q: How do you know if there's a dinosaur hiding under your bed?
A: Your nose is probably touching the ceiling.

Q: What keeps the ocean clean?
A: Mermaids.

Q: Why did the queen go to the dentist?
A: She went to get crowns put on her teeth.

Q: Why was the road angry?
A: Someone crossed it.

Q: What kind of trees have the best bark?
A: Dogwood trees.

**Q: What did the tooth fairy use to fix
her broken wand?**
A: Toothpaste.

**Q: What kind of flowers make
the best friends?**
A: Rosebuds.

Q: What kind of beans don't grow in a garden?
A: Jelly beans.

Q: Why did the bed wear a disguise?
A: It was undercover.

**Q: Why did the cow bring a hammer
to bed with him?**
A: Because he wanted to hit the hay.

Q: Why can't banks keep secrets?
A: They have too many tellers.

Q: What is the cheapest way to travel?
A: By sale-boat.

Q: What type of books do skunks usually read?
A: Best-smellers!

Q: What did Tennessee?

A: The same thing as Arkansas.

Q: Why are fish so bad at basketball?

A: They don't like getting close to the net.

Q: How do you communicate with fish?

A: You drop it a line.

Q: How do starfish communicate underwater?

A: On their shell phones.

Q: What do you call a dinosaur that is afraid of everything?

A: A nervous-rex.

Q: What do you call a cow that is afraid of everything?

A: A cow-ard.

Q: How does a gingerbread man make his bed?
A: With a cookie sheet.

Q: What do birds do before a workout?
A: They worm-up.

Knock, knock
Who's there?
Butter.
Butter who?
Butter not tell you. It's a secret.

Q: Why are horses so negative?

A: They say neigh to everything.

Q: What kind of vegetable has the worst manners?

A: A rude-abaga.

Q: Why was the bird at the library?

A: He was looking for bookworms.

Q: Why was the library busy?
A: It was overbooked.

Q: Why couldn't the fish go shopping?
A: It didn't have anemone.

Q: How many months have twenty-eight days?
A: Twelve.

Q: What is the coolest vegetable?
A: Radishes.

Q: What do trees eat for breakfast?
A: Oakmeal.

Q: Waiter, this food tastes kind of funny?
A: Then why aren't you laughing!

Q: Why are atoms untrustworthy?
A: Because they make up everything.

Q: What do frogs have with their cheeseburgers?
A: French flies and a croak.

Q: How do fleas travel from one dog to another?
A: They itch-hike.

Q: What do you call a pumpkin that looks out for you?

A: A body gourd.

Q: Why did the book go to the hospital?

A: To have its appendix removed.

Q: Why can't you believe anything a hippo says?

A: Because they tend to be hippo-crites.

Q: Why did the monkey go to the golf course?
A: To practice his swing.

Q: How did the tuba call the trumpet?
A: On his saxo-phone.

Q: What kind of photos do dentists take?
A: Tooth pics.

**Q: What kind of shoes do frogs wear
in the summer?**
A: Open-toad shoes.

**Q: What kind of sea creature needs
help with school?**
A: A *C* horse.

**Q: Why don't you want to get into
a fight with a snail?**
A: It might try to slug you.

Q: Where does a shark go on Saturday nights?
A: To the dive-in theater.

**Q: Why can't you win an argument
with a pencil?**
A: It's always write.

**Q: What do you call a guy stuffed in
your mailbox?**
A: Bill.

Q: What is a drummer's favorite vegetable?
A: Beets.

Q: What do you get when you cross a daisy and a bicycle?
A: Bike petals.

Q: What kind of bird is very wealthy?
A: An ost-rich.

Q: Where's the best place to keep an angry dog?
A: The *grrrr*age.

Q: What is the cleanest state?
A: Wash-ington.

Q: How do crocodiles like to cook their food?
A: In a crock-pot.

Q: What happens when you throw your vegetables in the ocean?

A: You get sea cucumbers.

Q: Why was the cow embarrassed?

A: It became a laughing stock.

Q: How can you learn more about spiders?

A: Check out their website.

Q: What kind of fish comes out at night?
A: A starfish.

Q: Why is jelly so much fun?
A: Because it's always jamming.

Q: Why are magicians great students?
A: They're good with trick questions.

Q. How do you make a tissue dance?

A: You put a little boogie in it!

Q: Why are bananas such good drivers?

A: They always keep their eyes peeled.

Q: Why was the photographer sentenced as guilty?

A: Her prints were all over the scene of the crime.

Q: What do bears wear in their hair?
A: Bearettes.

Q: Why was the shark always bragging?
A: He was fishing for compliments.

Q: Why was the bird always crying?
A: He was a blue bird.

Q: Why did the billboard go to the doctor?
A: It had a sign-us infection.

Knock, knock
Who's there?
Nose.
Nose who?
**Nobody nose a good joke when
they hear one anymore.**

Knock, knock

Who's there?

Whale.

Whale who?

Whale you tell me another knock-knock joke?

Knock, knock

Who's there?

Dawn.

Dawn who?

**It just dawned on me that I should
tell another joke.**

Q: What did the snail say on the turtle's back?
A: Wheeeeeeee!!

Q: What's black and white and black and white and black and white?
A: A penguin doing somersaults down a hill!

Q: How should a frog get out of a paper bag?
A: Riiiiiiip-it.

Q: Which month has 28 days?
A: They all do!

Q: What word is always spelled wrong?
A: Wrong.

Q: What has two hands but can't clap?
A: A clock.

Q: What gets damper as it dries?
A: A towel.

Q: What did Mama cow say to Baby cow?
A: It's pasture bedtime.

**Q: What has four legs, one head,
and only one foot?**
A: A bed.

Q: Can a frog jump higher than the Empire State Building?

A: Of course, the Empire State Building can't jump.

Q: Who always sleeps with their shoes on?
A: Horses

Q: What can you never eat for breakfast?
A: Lunch and dinner

Q: What can you maintain without saying anything?
A: Silence.

Q: **What is really easy to get into but difficult to get out of?**
A: Trouble.

A dad bought a donkey for his son because he thought he might get a kick out of it.

Q: What is difficult to keep, hold, or destroy?
A: A secret

**Q: A boy fell off a 20-foot ladder.
He wasn't hurt. Why?**
A: He fell off the bottom step.

**Q: What has two words, starts with P, ends
with E, and has thousands of letters?**
A: Post Office

Q: What animal asks too many questions?
A: An owl

The best way to stop a charging bull
is to take away his credit card.

Q: What is something you can catch
but you can't throw it?
A: A cold.

A chicken crossing the road is poultry
in motion.

Q: What type of room has no doors?
A: A mushroom.

Q: When is homework no longer homework?
A: When you turn it in to the teacher.

**Q: Railroad. How do you spell
that without any R's?**
A: T-H-A-T

Q: What's black and white and red all over?

A: An embarrassed zebra.

Q: What can travel around the world but
stays in the corner?

A: A stamp.

Q: What is larger than you but weighs nothing?

A: Your shadow.

Q: Why are calendars so busy?

A: They have a lot of dates.

I couldn't figure out how lightning worked and then it struck me.

He's been to the dentist on many occasions so he knew the drill.

Q: What goes up but never comes back down?
A: Your age.

Q: What is the slipperiest country?
A: Greece!

Q: What occurs twice in one moment, once in
a millennium, but never in a hundred years?
A: The letter M.

It was an emotional wedding.
Even the cake was in tiers.

Q: What has a head and a tail but no legs?
A: A penny.

Chalkboards are remarkable.

Q: Which side of the dog has the most hair?
A: The outside.

Time flies like an arrow but fruit flies
like a banana.

Q: What do you find at the end of a rainbow?
A: W!

Q: What's a snake's favorite subject in school?
A: Hissstory.

Q: What touches every continent but has no beginning, middle, or end?
A: The Ocean.

Q: What never asks a question but needs an answer?
A: A telephone.

Q: Why are brooms always late?
A: They usually oversweep.

Q: What do ghosts wear on their feet?
A: BOO-ts.

Q: What can go up and down without moving?
A: Stairs.

Q: What must you break before you can use it?
A: An egg.

Q: What do you throw away when you want to use it?
A: An anchor.

Q: What is full of keys but can't open any doors?
A: A piano.

Exit signs. They're on the way out.

Q: What has no life but can still die?
A: A battery.

Q: What will die if you give it water?
A: Fire.

Q: How many apples can you fit in an empty box?
A: None! If you put apples in it, the box won't be empty anymore.

Q: What word is shorter when you add two letters to it?
A: Short.

Q: What is as big as a dinosaur but weighs less than a dinosaur?

A: A dinosaur's shadow.

Q: **What is yours but gets used by others more?**
A: Your name.

Q: **What shows up at night and disappears in the day time but you can always find in Hollywood?**
A: Stars.

Q: **What's one way to double your money?**
A: Put it front of a mirror.

Q: What do you hold without touching it?
A: A conversation.

Q: What insect can you spell with one letter?
A: Bee.

Q: What is the capital of Hawaii?
A: H.

Q: When is the moon the heaviest?
A: When it's full.

Q: What can run but can't walk?
A: A river.

Q: What do people and animals make but you can't see?
A: Noise.

**Q: What has a back and four legs
but no body?**
A: A chair.

He tried to catch fog but mist.

Q: What kind of coach has no wheels?
A: A baseball coach.

Q: What kind of tree do you find in the kitchen?
A: A pantry.

Q: What ten-letter word starts with g-a-s?
A: Automobile.

Q: What time is the same spelled both forward and backwards?
A: Noon.

Q: Where will you always find money?

A: In the dictionary.

Q: If money grew on trees, what would everyone's favorite season be?
A: Fall.

Q: Why is Rudolph the Red Nosed Reindeer so good at trivia?
A: He NOSE a lot.

Once you've seen one shopping center, you've seen a mall.

Q: Why did the farmer plant a light bulb?

A: He wanted to grow a power plant.

Long stories about knights tend to dragon.

Q: How did Benjamin Franklin feel after he discovered electricity?

A: He was shocked.

Q: What does a nuclear scientist do in her spare time?

A: Goes fission.

Q: What is burned by cars that are driven at night?

A: The midnight oil.

Q: When you're looking for a lost remote, why is it always in the last place you looked?

A: Because once you find it, you stop looking.

Q: **What thrives in winter, dies in summer,
and its roots grow upward?**
A: An icicle.

Q: How can a person go 7 days without sleep?
A: He or she only sleeps at night.

**Q: What has four fingers and one thumb
but is not alive?**
A: A glove.

Q: What is as light as air but something that even the strongest person can't hold for more than five minutes?

A: Breath.

Q: Name three consecutive days without saying Wednesday, Friday, or Sunday.
A: Yesterday, today, and tomorrow.

Q: What has three feet but cannot walk, dance, or run?
A: A yardstick.

Q: A man is running a marathon and passes the person in second place, what place is he now in?
A: Second place.

**Q: Which vegetable can your father
make with Scissors?**
A: Pa snips.

Q: What is full of holes but still holds water?
A: A sponge.

Q: If dogs have fleas, what do sheep have?
A: Fleece.

**Q: What starts out tall but gets shorter
the longer it stands?**
A: A candle.

Q: What side of the rabbit has the most fur?
A: The outside.

Q: What is broken with only one word?
A: Silence.

Q: Did you hear the joke about the roof?
A: Never mind, it's over your head!

Q: What has six legs but only walks around on four?
A: A rider on her horse.

Q: What is always on its way but never arrives?
A: Tomorrow.

Q: What has no beginning or end and nothing in the middle?

A: A doughnut.

Q: Do you know how expensive mixed nuts are?

A: Very. It costs an almond a leg.

He used to have a fear of hurdles until one day he got over it.

Q: What is red when it's in use, black when
it's not, and gray when you throw it out?
A: Coal.

Being struck by lightning is a
shocking experience.

Q: What do you bring out on the table
to cut but never eat?
A: A deck of cards.

Q: Why do you never see dragons out during the day?

A: Because they like to hunt knights.

Q: What do you think is the most popular use of cowhide?

A: To cover cows, of course.

Q: What does a dog have that no other animal has?

A: Puppies!

Q: When is it possible for Friday to come before Thursday?

A: In the dictionary.

There was once a blanket factory in town,
but the company folded.

Q: What building has the most stories?
A: A library.

Q: What can you sit on, sleep on,
and brush your teeth with?
A: A chair, a bed, and a toothbrush.

Q: Where's the best place to buy pens?
A: Pennsylvania.

Q: Who can shave over twenty times a day and still have a beard?
A: A barber.

Q: Four children and two dogs weren't standing under an umbrella so how did none of them get wet?
A: It wasn't raining.

**Q: What can you keep after
giving to someone else?**
A: A promise.

**Q: What do you always answer
without a question?**
A: A telephone.

A perfectly spherical pumpkin makes good pi.

**Q: What can you put in your pocket
that keeps it empty?**
A: A hole.

Q: What is tiny and sharp and has one eye?
A: A needle.

Q: What is there a lot of in the Pacific Ocean?
A: Water.

Q: What looks like half of an apple?
A: The other half.

Q: Where do wealthy people eat their poultry?
A: In the chicken wing.

People who eat candy with two hands are ambi-dextrose.

Q: What is the first thing Elizabeth I did when she came to the throne?

A: Sit on it.

Q: Why do you have to go to bed?
A: Because your bed won't come to you!

Q: What is a disastrous cat called?
A: A catastrophe.

Q: Why is it a bad idea to tell a joke while you're playing ice hockey?
A: Because the ice might crack up.

I was going to tell you a funny joke about a boomerang but I forgot. I'm sure it will come back to me.

Q: How did the portrait end up in police custody?
A: It was framed.

Q: What runs and whistles but can't walk or talk?
A: A train.

**Q: Why can leopards never escape
from the zoo?**

A: They are always spotted.

Q: Why are boats and shops alike?
A: One has sails and the other has sales.

Q: What gets older but doesn't age?
A: A portrait

Q: What's hard to maintain but easily broken?
A: Silence.

Q: **What do you call a small wound?**
A: A short cut.

I wanted to look for my missing watch but I couldn't find the time.

Q: **Why does a Moon-rock taste better than an Earth-rock?**
A: Because it's a little meteor.

Q: When is a ring square?

A: When it's a boxing ring.

She tried to eat a clock but it was very time consuming.

Q: What would you call a pun sandwich?

A: A Punini

Q: What does a winner lose in a race?
A: His breath.

Q: Why did the cow lie down in the grass?
A: He was ground beef.

Q: What has thirty heads and thirty tails?
A: Thirty quarters.

Q: What can you see better as it gets darker?
A: Stars.

**Q: What starts with T, ends with T,
and is full of T?**
A: A teapot.

**Q: What has wings and can fly
but is not a bird or an insect?**
A: A plane.

Q: What can you never hold in your right hand?
A: Your right hand.

Q: What kind of coat is always wet when you put it on?
A: A coat of paint.

Q: How many seconds are there in one year?

A: 12

- January 2nd
- February 2nd
- March 2nd
- April 2nd
- May 2nd
- June 2nd
- July 2nd
- August 2nd
- September 2nd
- October 2nd
- November 2nd
- December 2nd

Q: What do you call a bear without an ear?

A: A "b"

Q: What's the most curious letter?
A: Y.

Q: The man who made it doesn't want it. The man who bought it doesn't need it. The man who needs it doesn't know it. What is it?
A: A coffin.

Q: What does December have that the other months don't have?
A: The letter D.

Q: What does down but never comes up?

A: Rain

Q: What type of tree can you carry in your hand?

A: A palm.

Q: What can go up a chimney but can't go down a chimney up?

A: An umbrella.

Q: If you are what you eat, what should you stay away from?
A: The nuts.

Q: How do you make the number one vanish?
A: Add a "G" to it and it's gone!

Q: What has a neck but not a head?
A: A bottle.

Q: What is something you can hear but not see or touch?

A: Your voice.

Q: What goes uphill and downhill but always stays in the same place?

A: A road.

Q: Why did the man put a clock in a safe?

A: He wanted to save time.

Q: **Which letter of the alphabet is not me?**
A: U.

Q: How is the letter "A" like noon?
A: It's right in the middle of the day.

Q: Which letter of the alphabet would you say is the fullest of water?
A: The letter "C"

Q: What's as big as a horse but doesn't weigh anything?
A: A horse's shadow.

To write with a broken pencil is pointless.

Q: What are the two strongest days of the week?
A: Saturday and Sunday—the rest are weak days.

Oranges are very a-peeling.

Q: What's the difference between electricity and lightning?
A: You don't have to pay for lightning.

Q: Why are baseball stadiums so cool?
A: There's a fan in every seat.

People love crazy glue.
They're very attached to it.

Q: What has waves but isn't the ocean?
A: Hair.

Q: What has teeth but can't bite?
A: A comb.

Q: What falls but never breaks?
A: Night.

The old batteries were distributed free of charge.

Q: What breaks but never falls?
A: Day.

Q: What will break if it falls?
A: Glass.

Q: Which letter of the alphabet stings?
A: B.

**Q: What loses its head in the morning
and gets it back at night?**
A: A pillow.

Yesterday a clown held the door open for someone. It was a nice jester.

Q: What asks but never answers?
A: An owl.

Q: During what month do people sleep the least?
A: February—it's the shortest.

**Q: Who builds bridges of silver
and crowns of gold?**
A: A dentist.

He couldn't quite understand the angle his math teacher was going for.

Q: What has six eyes but can't see anything?
A: The three blind mice.

Q: What kind of make-up do ghosts wear?
A: Mas-SCARE-a!

Glass windows are such a pane.

**Q: What type of sea creature can help
you build a house?**
A: A hammerhead shark.

**Q: What has forests with no trees, rivers
without water, roads without cars,
and deserts without sand?**
A: A map.

**He didn't like his beard at first
but then it grew on him.**

Q: What can you break easily without ever touching it or seeing it?
A: A promise.

Q: Why do sharks only swim in salt water?
A: Pepper water makes them sneeze.

Q: What do you call a cat with one leg?
A: A cat.

Q: The more you take, the more you leave behind. What is it?

A: Footsteps.

Q: What do you throw away when you want to use and take in when you want to use it?

A: An anchor.

Q: What will always come but never arrive today?

A: Tomorrow.

Q: What goes around all cities and towns but never comes inside?

A: Streets.

Q: What has no life but can die?

A: A battery.

Q: What is always answered but never asks a question?

A: A doorbell.

Q: **What has a lot of memories
but owns nothing?**
A: A picture frame.

Q: **What goes up when water comes down?**
A: An umbrella.

Q: **What's the day after yesterday?**
A: Today!

**Q: What's the worst thing about throwing
a party in space?**
A: You have to planet!

Jackhammers. They're groundbreaking.

**Q: What occurs twice in a week,
once in a year, but never in a day?**
A: The letter "e"

Q: How do you make antifreeze?

A: You take away her sweater!

A gossip is someone with a great
sense of rumor.

**Q: Which word in the dictionary is always
spelled incorrectly?**
A: Incorrectly.

Q: How do you make fruit punch?
A: Put an apple in a boxing glove.

Vinyl records.
They're groovy.

Q: What does a spy do when he gets cold?
A: He goes undercover.

Q: Why are rivers always rich?
A: Because they have two banks.

Q: What turns without moving?
A: Milk. It can turn sour.

Q: What part of your body has the most rhythm?
A: Eardrums.

Past, present, and future were hanging out. It was tense.

Q: How is the letter "E" like London?

A: Because "E" is the capital of England.

**Q: How many apples can you fit in
an empty box?**

A: Zero. If you put an apple in it,
it won't be empty anymore.

**If towels could tell jokes they would
probably have a dry sense of humor.**

Q: Did you hear about the guy who got a brain transplant?

A: He wasn't going to originally get it but changed his mind.

Q: What happened when the comedian tried to tell a chemistry joke?

A: She didn't get a reaction.

Q: What happened to the girl reading the book on anti-gravity?

A: It was impossible to put down.

It's hard to explain puns to a kleptomaniac.
They always take everything literally.

His fear of heights has elevated his heartrate.

Q: Did you hear about the guy who got fired
from the calendar factory?
A: All he did was take a day off.

Q: **If there are three apples and you take away two, how many do you have?**
A: Two.

Q: **What can fill up a room but take up no space?**
A: Light.

Q: **What falls but never gets hurt?**
A: Snow.

He went to a seafood disco last week
and pulled a mussel.

Q: What has a tongue but cannot talk?
A: A shoe.

Q: What has one eye and cannot see?
A: A needle.

When a clock is hungry it always goes back for seconds.

Q: When is the best time to eat eggs?
A: The crack of dawn.

Q: Does your shirt have holes in it?
A: No, then how did you put it on?

Q: What is a plumber's favorite shoe?
A: Clogs.

Q: What do you call chandeliers?
A: High lights.

Math teachers who retire call it the "aftermath."

Q: What time is it when the clock strikes 13?
A: Time to get a new clock.

The person who invented the door knock must have won the no-bell prize.

Q: How do Vikings communicate?
A: Norse code.

The thief who stole the calendar
got twelve months.

Q: Which day do chickens hate the most?
A: Fry-day

Q: Why did the lobster cross the road?
A: To get to the other tide.

**Q: What do you call a dinosaur
with a big vocabulary?**
A: A thesaurus.

Q: What do you call an alligator in a vest?
A: An investigator.

Q: How far can a fox run into a field?
A: Halfway. And then he's running out of it.

Q: **How many bananas can you eat
on an empty stomach?**

A: Just one. After that it's not empty anymore.

Q: What does an orthodontist do in a fight?

A: He braces himself.

Q: Why did the builder hate glass windows?

A: Glass windows are such a pane.

Q: What can you never eat for lunch?
A: Breakfast or dinner!

Q: Where is the ocean the deepest?
A: The bottom.

Q: How is the letter A like a flower?
A: Because the B is always after it.

Q: **What do you call a dish masquerading as Italian food?**
A: Impasta!

Q: **What has four fingers and a thumb but isn't living?**
A: A glove.

Q: **What can be swallowed but can also swallow you?**
A: Pride.

Q: What's made of wood but can't be sawed?
A: Saw dust.

Q: What side of the cat has the most fur?
A: The outside.

Q: Why was 6 so mad at 7?
A: Because 7 8 9.

Q: What has ten letters and starts with gas?
A: An automobile.

Q: How many apples grow on trees?
A: All apples grow on trees.

Q: Why can't a T-Rex clap?
A: Because they are extinct.

Q: How do you make seven even?
A: Take away the S.

Instead of being sad he was delighted when the batteries in his flashlight went out.

Q: What has a foot but no leg?
A: A ruler.

Her fear of moving stairs is escalating.

Q: What is the coolest letter of the alphabet?
A: B. It's always surrounded by AC.

Eggs are terrible comedians. They always crack up at their own jokes.

Q: What animal likes to learn?
A: Fish, they travel in schools!

Q: What would you call a fish with a missing eye?
A: A fish.

Q: What do you call a fancy fish?
A: Sofishticated.

Q: Why was the broom late?
A: It overswept.

Without geometry, life is pointless.

Knock knock.
Who's there?
Olive.
Olive who?
Olive YOU!

Q: Why is the calendar so popular?
A: Because it has so many dates.

Math teachers have a lot of problems.

Q: Why do you go to bed every night?
A: Because the bed won't come to you.

Q: What do lawyers wear to court?
A: Lawsuits.

Q: Why did the little pigs fall asleep when grandpa told a story?
A: Because Grandpa was a boar.

Q: What do you get when you cross an apple with a Christmas tree?
A: A pineapple.

Q: How do you make the number one disappear?
A: Add a G to it and it's gone.

Bananas are one of the most appealing fruits.

People who believe in ghosts are very ghoulable.

Q: What do Pandas have that no other animal has?

A: Baby pandas.

Q: What did 0 say to 8?

A: "Nice belt."

Q: What happened to the guy who had his whole left side removed?

A: He was all right.

Q: How do celebrities stay cool?
A: They have a lot of fans.

Q: Who walks into a restaurant, wastes shoots and leaves?
A: A panda

Q: Which hand is better to write with?
A: Neither. It's better to use a pen or a pencil.

Q: What can even the most careful person overlook?

A: Their nose.

Q: What is the capital of Alaska?

A: A.

A boiled egg for breakfast is hard to beat.

Q: What did Delaware?

A: Her New Jersey.

Q: Why is England the wettest country?

A: Because the queen has reigned there for years.

Q: Where was the Declaration of Independence signed?

A: On the bottom.

Simple as 3.14

Q: How can sea captains use amphibians?
A: As froghorns.

Some river valleys are absolutely gorges.

Q: How many sides does a circle have?
A: Two. Inside and outside.

She stayed up all night to see where the sun went and then it dawned on her.

He started working at a bakery because he kneaded dough.

Q: Why did the giraffes get bad grades?
A: She had her head in the clouds.

A backwards poet writes inverse.

Every calendar's days are numbered.

Q: What musical is about a train conductor?
A: "My Fare Lady"

Q: Why do ambassadors never get sick?
A: Diplomatic immunity.

Q: Why did the robber shower before she robbed a bank?
A: She wanted to make a clean getaway.

Q: Why did the man run around his bed?
A: He was trying to catch up on sleep.

Q: Why don't traffic lights go swimming?
A: Because they take too long to change.

Q: What does even the most careful person overlook?
A: Their nose.

Q: Why was the belt arrested?

A: Because it held up a pair of pants.

Q: What's the difference between a TV and a newspaper?

A: Have you ever tried to swat a fly with a TV?

Q: What did the paper say to the pencil?

A: Write on!

Q: Why can't you tell an egg a joke?
A: Because it might crack up.

Q: What can be full but never overflow?
A: The moon.

Q: What can you keep after giving it to someone else?
A: Your word.

Q: What goes around the wood but never goes into the wood?
A: The rings of a tree.

Q: What is a cat's favorite dessert?
A: Mice Cream!

He tried to look for his missing clock but couldn't find the time.

Q: What walks all day on its head?
A: A nail in a horseshoe.

Q: What has 13 hearts but no other organs?
A: A deck of playing cards.

She used to hate math until she realized decimals had a point.

Q: What dies but can be brought back to life with a simple charge?
A: A battery.

Q: What lives without a body, hears without ears, and speaks without a mouth?
A: An echo.

Q: Who always has a date?
A: A Calendar.

Q: What part of the snake is musical?
A: The scales.

Q: What can you never eat for dinner?
A: Breakfast or lunch.

**Q: What is the beginning of eternity
and the end of time and space?**
A: The letter E.

Q: Why does lightning shock people?
A: Because it doesn't know how to conduct itself.

Q: How do hens feel on Mondays?
A: Eggshausted.

Q: What falls but never hits the ground?
A: The temperature.

Q: What kind of awards do dentists get?
A: Plaques.

Q: What does a dentist do during
an earthquake?

A: She braces herself.

Q: Why did the tree go to the dentist?

A: To get a root canal.

Q: What stands on one leg with
its heart on its head?

A: Cabbage.

Q: What is full of holes but holds water?
A: A sponge.

Q: What goes up the stairs even though it doesn't move?
A: A rug.

Puns about ants bug me.

She had a photographic memory
but never developed it.

Q: When prices go up,
what remains stationary?
A: Writing paper and envelopes.

Q: What kind of can doesn't
need a can opener?
A: A pelican.

Q: What is the best month for a parade?
A: March!

Q: Why was the picture sent to jail?
A: Because it was framed.

Q: Where was the pencil store located?
A: Pennsylvania

**Q: What do you get when you
pour cement on a thief?**

A: A hardened criminal.

**Closing the window to keep the bugs
out is such a pane.**

**Q: What five-letter word sounds the same if
you take away the first and last letter?**

A: Empty.

Q: What word is smaller when you
add two letters to it?
A: Small.

You can usually bank on a river full of fish.

Q: What road vehicle has four wheels
and flies?
A: A garbage truck.

Q: What has four legs, a head, and a foot?
A: A bed.

Q: Where does a trout deposit his money?
A: A riverbank.

Q: Why do ghosts like to haunt libraries?
A: They like being around the BOOks.

Q: Can February March?
A: No, but April May.

Everyone was so tired on April 1st.
They had just finished a March of 31 days.

Q: What is it that after you take away the
whole some still remains?
A: Wholesome.

ARE YOU A MINECRAFT FAN IN NEED OF A GOOD LAUGH?

Check out our Minecraft joke books!

Write Your Own Jokes Here!

_____

_____

_____

_____

_____

_____

_____

_____

_____

_____

_____

_____

_____

_____

Write Your Own Jokes Here!

_____

_____

_____

_____

_____

_____

_____

_____

_____

_____

_____

_____

_____

_____

_____

Write Your Own Jokes Here!

_____

_____

_____

_____

_____

_____

_____

_____

_____

_____

_____

_____

_____

_____

_____

Write Your Own Jokes Here!

Write Your Own Jokes Here!

_____

_____

_____

_____

_____

_____

_____

_____

_____

_____

_____

_____

_____

_____

Write Your Own Jokes Here!

Write Your Own Jokes Here!

_____

_____

_____

_____

_____

_____

_____

_____

_____

_____

_____

_____

_____

Write Your Own Jokes Here!

_____

_____

_____

_____

_____

_____

_____

_____

_____

_____

_____

_____

_____

_____

_____

_____

Write Your Own Jokes Here!

_____

_____

_____

_____

_____

_____

_____

_____

_____

_____

_____

_____

_____

_____

Write Your Own Jokes Here!